SWIM

You've gotta swim-
don't let yourself sink.
Just find the horizon
I promise you it's not
as far as you think.

--Lyrics from *Swim,* by Jack's Mannequin (2008)

Preface

I tread cautiously when writing about mental illness, as I never want to falsely portray or romanticize it. As a complete disclaimer, a few of the things I write about are not things I have experienced directly, but through friends and family very close to me. In talking with them and being with them through these struggles, I felt I could do the topics justice for them and for anyone who may be living them.

As for eating disorders, anxiety and OCD, I write from my own personal experience.

I say all of this because although it is important to me to never glamorize or misrepresent a struggle I have not had, it is also my goal to give voice to and spread awareness about as many aspects of mental illness and wellness as I can.

If you struggle with mental illness, I want you to keep fighting and I hope these words help you in some way. I hope you enjoy this book as much as I enjoyed writing it.

xoxo, Emily

For all who have wanted to leave
but have chosen to stay.
And fight.

Contents

How do you know you are a goddess?

I cried oceans, but did not drown.

x

PART 1

(Bad Science)

My therapist tells me
to draw my OCD
and hang it on my fridge
so I can look it in the eye everyday
and stop running.

I give the bastard
ten tentacles
and putrid, rotting flesh.
Brown, black, green;
Crayola doesn't even make
the color of its skin.

The tentacles wrap around me
inside me
under and over me
like a forest of thorny vines
over quicksand.

That's pretty terrifying
someone says
but they have *no* idea.

Nobody does.

--OCD VI

The mental illnesses
were all together at a party
the first time somebody said
misery loves company
and they took it way,
way too seriously.

-A bad joke

I choke on words
like hard candy
swallowed too soon
and they get stuck.
You can squeeze my stomach
and pound my back
until we are both blue in the face,
but I will not cough them up.

-Choke

My eyes scan the room
and I get a strange feeling in my gut;
it's happening again.
Everything is the right color
and in the right place
but it's almost too perfect,
like a movie set
or wallpaper.
You're there too, but
dream-you and you-you are too similar to tell apart
so I pinch myself and thank God I feel it.

Maybe I'm awake after all
or maybe this is just
what the man in the white coat meant by
vivid.

--Zoloft dreams

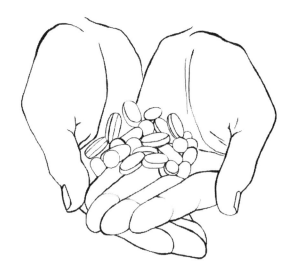

Just think how much better you have it than most;
be positive.

Have you tried yoga?

Maybe you just need some sun,

they say
as if any of that will improve
a chemical imbalance;
that's just bad science.

--Bad science

She wrung her hands
the way you would a wet towel
but nothing dripped out.
You see,
anxiety cannot be
squeezed out of a person
like bath water.

-*Bath water*

I wonder what it's like
to live in a head
that performs like a
well-synchronized
orchestra,
because under my skull
is a noisy,
out of tune piano
with broken strings
and ten missing keys.

--OCD VII

I was falling down the waterfall
panicking, flailing,
while tourists with cameras
admired it from the riverbank,
in awe of its beauty.

You see, perspective is everything.

--What I feel like to me/What I look like to them

I used to envy people who could pick up a knife
and not think to themselves *what if I stabbed someone?*

I watched them cut their steaks
so mindlessly,
so unafraid.

Fork in meat,
cut, cut, cut.
fork in mouth,
repeat.
Sometimes I got soup
just because I didn't need a little weapon to eat it.

Eating shouldn't be this hard,
life shouldn't be this hard,
and don't even get me started with scissors.
All of these people cutting their steaks and
doing their construction paper projects;
I must be crazy, because nobody else has these
thoughts
these bloody thoughts
these *what if I killed my sister* thoughts.

I once stayed awake for thirty-six hours
crying and avoiding sharp things
 because what if I did it in my sleep?

--OCD VIII

11

Don't you love me?
Don't you know I love you?

--Things not say to someone with suicidal ideation

Put down some of your load,
and tell me what I can carry.

--What to say instead

Don't try to fix what isn't broken.

> The problem is, I can never tell if something is
> actually broken, or if I'm just afraid it is.

> *--Health anxiety*

I did not choose to be this way;
nervous all the time
like a fox-hunted rabbit.
Prepared,
like Prometheus,
to have my liver ripped out
every night by a taloned eagle,
always ready for the pain.
It's not pessimism,
it's just the way I'm wired
and I can't change it
and you can't fix it.

--You can't

Hunger bubbles up
like molten lava
and makes me powerful,
so powerful;
like a phoenix
like a resurrection
like losing the parts of me
I did not want
to please the fiery goddess
who goes by 'Ana' for short.

--Freshman year

Look at all of those people,
stuck in wooden ships
being tossed and
turned by the treacherous sea.
How I envy them,
for depression
is being stuck in the same sea
in a boat without sails.

Understand why I do not have the hope
you conjure so easily.

--A ship without sails

Some girls break so evenly
as if they came out of the womb
with perforations.
But I rip like old love letters;
to pieces on the floor,
covered in tears.

--Perforations

Insecurities,
mirrors,
and fear.
Maybe I have always felt too heavy
because this body was not meant
to carry such a weight.

--Dysmorphia

Fresh-squeezed grapefruit
because it's *healthy*
never mind that it only has 52 calories
-who's counting-
Lunch is for the weak;
I get satisfaction from
one of those knockoff cappuccinos
in the dining hall.
It's probably bad for me
but it goes right through
like liquid down a pipe that's just been plunged.
Dinner?
Oh, no thank you,
I already ate.

Late at night
the cravings come
so I go out and buy a chocolate bar
or maybe a donut
and just to prove I'm strong
I throw it all away and
wash my hands of the almost-deed.
Pride courses through my veins
like the nutrients I've learned to live without.
It's not that hard; it's just will power.

And I can stop anytime I want.

--Starve

20

If they cut for attention,
then why do they
hide
their scars?

--Cut

The sky howls like a banshee
and I feel a storm in my bones,
but no one believes me.

A tornado rips through
the cat vomit sky
and the oak tree shrieks and crashes down,
crushing her little body
like it does every time.
I'm screaming
but no one can hear it
over the sky's sick laughter
and torrents of the wind.

--Zoloft dreams II

22

One of the most wicked things
anyone ever said to me was
our thoughts become us.

  --OCD IX

Tangled up
like earbuds or yarn
or necklaces that've been in my jewelry box
since childhood.
My stomach is bunched up
in a million knots
and you think *just getting out of bed*
will make this better?

--More bad science

I heard this girl
no more than twelve
sobbing in a dressing room
about her stretch marks
and her mother said

I will buy you the cream,
and they will go away
but you have *to use it-it's expensive.*

That day, a child learned
that a part of her
needed getting rid of
and that it was worth
paying money to make happen.

--How it begins (a completely true story)

25

It may have devoured your dreams,
but look how sick they are making it.
Little dove,
reach your hand
into its hot, stinking belly
and take them back
for yourself.

--You will beat this

If all you did this year
was walk away
from something that was
sucking the life from your
too-frail bones,
that is movement enough.

--Movement

Learn to be okay
with being content
and happiness
will fall into your hands
like rain
into a desert
that has accepted
the sun.

--Content

I am afraid
of losing loved ones
and being alone in the dark
but mostly
I am afraid of being
merely tolerated
when I want so badly
to be loved.

--*Insecure*

Raw knuckles,
bloodshot eyes
and stolen laxatives.
All easy to miss
when hidden
behind a pretty smile
(admittedly less white these days)
some baggy clothes
and a few poorly-thought out lies.

--*Purge*

You look so put together
but you're cracking to pieces.
Your hands don't feel like your hands
and it's hard to recognize
the touch of your own skin
or the taste of your mouth.

You're swimming up by the ceiling,
your feet are rooted on the ground
and your head is stuck
somewhere in between.
It's scary but it won't last forever.

Float

and know that gravity
will always bring you back
to yourself.

-- Dp/Dr (for Edvina)

31

Your skin bruises like a peach
but it's smooth and even
because sometimes the black and blue shows up
in other ways.

In tears in your pillow at one a.m.
when he's just texted
"I'm sorry"
before ghosting for three days
when you know he is with *her.*

In the welts that rise between you and your family
because you're constantly forced to choose him over them
because that's love, *right?*

In the swelling in the pit of your heart each day
when you're trying to figure out if he's going to be there or
not.

In your broken self-esteem;
broken because whenever he does something wrong,
it is somehow your fault.

Your whole body is battered
and hemorrhaging and patched up
with bloody bandages you crafted yourself
because no doctor would believe he's hurting you.

Because these deep wounds;
they don't leave a scratch.

--Emotional abuse

Everyone around me
seemed so happy
that when you asked how I was
I smiled and said
good
because I wanted to fit in
with all the other liars.

--*How have you been*

At least when you break a horse,
it knows what's happening.

You broke me without whips or cages,
without raised voices or fists.
Just a hand on the small of my back,
control disguised as care,
guiding me everywhere
I did not want to go.

--*Emotional abuse II*

We think of ourselves
 to be these great trapeze artists,
balancing school and love and friends,
work and sex and babies.

But the tightrope will never steady
until we learn to take care of ourselves.

--Circus

I cannot tell who is to blame;
the doctors,
insurance companies,
or the system.
But somebody
should be held accountable
for everyone who tried to get help
when their head didn't feel quite right
and couldn't get more than five minutes
of the doctor's time.

--Help. Us.

I am a shell of who I used to be,
but hold me close
-listen-
and you will hear the tides
churning in my heart,
getting ready for a great swell.

--Listen

You have to understand
that every day is a victory,
and even if you do nothing but get out of bed
-even if you *don't* get out of bed-
you are still worthy
of the air in your lungs
and the time this life is giving you.

--Today is a victory

Black-lined eyes
staring into nothing.
Fourteen.
Bored and anxious all at once.
Too young to feel the hope of the future,
too old to remember
the soft warm winds of childhood.

She asks how it will ever get better
and I want to scream *it will, it will.*

Just know when your mind whispers
Nobody cares
that is great and terrible lie.

--Fourteen

39

I asked my mother
how to be like her;
steady like the ocean,
calm like the sea.
She said
remember child,
that all waves break
eventually
but the important thing
is to just keep swimming.

--Just keep swimming

PART 2

(Bruised)

antidote
(an-ti-doht)

1. A medicine or other remedy for counteracting the effects of poison, toxin, disease, etc.

2. Can be found in the forms of: activated charcoal, epi-pens, urinating on the jellyfish sting, poetry, sad songs, alcohol (though this is now thought to be more of a numbing agent than a cure), deleting old text messages, throwing away the shirts they left behind (yes, even the flannel one), buying new sheets, cleansing your palate (you know what I mean by this), and going to the places you used to go together to reclaim them for yourself.

Origin: 1400-1450 [Greek] *antidoton* (something to counteract)

You are going to watch him treat another woman better. From a distance, from second Instagram accounts no one knows you have, from looking at photographs you shouldn't just to "see how he is doing." You are going to see him bragging about her, posting perfect pictures he never took with you (remember these are staged). It will cut and burn and boil like hot, visceral blood. But you have to - *have to* - remember this is not a reflection of you. When you had him, he was a boy and somewhere along the way he started to learn how to be a man. Try to be happy that he isn't ripping her apart the way he did you.

Try to be glad that he has grown.

--Hard truths

I mixed cinnamon and honey
a sprig of rosemary
lavender essence
turmeric
and some ginger
boiled water
and made a potion
because the witch doctor
said it would cure anything
but my heart hurts just the same.

I guess I forgot to add the
thyme.

--Witch doctors and wordplay

If I had three hands
I would use one
to sow the earth beneath my feet,
one to tend to the ones I love
and one to care for myself.

But alas,
I have only two.

--*Three hands*

You say
I'm the one your father warned you about
as if I am seventeen
and it's still appealing
to fall in love with someone
my family would hate.

--It's not

Don't give him the power to hurt you,
they warn.
As if I intend to.
As if I'll have any choice in the matter.

--Useless advice

I staggered into you
like a man starving for water
in the Akobo.
Such a shame
you were little more
than a mirage.

--Desert

He says he admires me
but I am not a doll
made to be looked at and kept pretty
behind cheap packaging
on the highest shelf.

I am meant to be taken out
and played with.

--Not a doll

There was an irresistible indifference to you,
as if you knew you were just a speck of dust
on an inconsequential rock
floating through space and time,
and you were fine with it.

And I just wanted to float with you.

--Float

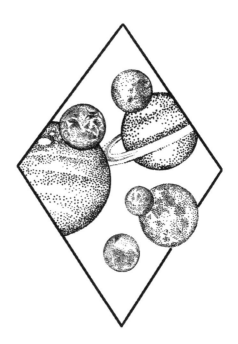

I drown in you
like the Indian Ocean
if the Indian Ocean were
a grey t-shirt and Old Spice.
Hands in my hair,
your chest rises and falls
in waves
that keep me steady
when I'm ten seconds from breaking.

You are the only ocean
I've ever been able to breathe under.

--Kel

It is true,
there are things
that should not be said aloud
for though I don't believe in censorship,
I do believe in kindness.

Your best friend is going to keep dating *that guy*
whether you approve or not.

Your sister isn't asking if the dress makes her look fat
because she actually wants to know;
she just wants a compliment like the rest of us.

And yes, of course I love you
but if I tell you it will only hurt us both.

I guard the truths coming out of my mouth
like Cerberus guards the underworld,
because I know some things will release
hell and Hades if they ever get out.

--Things we should not say aloud

Take the hammer
smash my bones and fingers
into a thousand pieces
just please,
please
leave my lungs alone.

--Don't take my breath away

If you have to give him
all of you
every part
every minute
every day
that isn't love.

Love is keeping some of you
for you.

--Keeping

I swallow you like bitter melon
dipped in thick, syrupy honey
indulging in your sweetness
regretting the aftertaste.

--I should have spit you out

You feel like you can't breathe without her
but you can, and you will.
And with new air
will come new cells
that do not know
the touch of her hands
or the taste of her mouth
or the scent of her skin.

And that may hurt,
but rebuilding wasn't meant
to be painless.

--Reconstruction

You dropped me
like a child
holding a glass cup
for the first time
not understanding
that once it falls,
it is gone forever.

--Don't spill it

I'm learning to fly slowly
from a book I hide
under my bed
and by watching
birds and bats and butterflies
secretly,
privately,
and when I finally fly away
you'll still be wondering
when I learned to open the window.

--Learn to Fly

I am always wary
of people who merely nibble
on dessert;
I don't want someone
who ruins a whole cookie
just to get a taste.

--*Eat the whole damn thing*

Some men
cannot love you
the way you want them to
because they learned how to love
from sometimes-parents
who blamed each other
and left every time something got hard.

Even so, it is not your job
to show them to the light.

-*Some men*

He took my hand and whispered
I'm not dangerous, I'm misunderstood
and I swear to God,
I almost believed him.

--Bad boy

I used to do this thing;
I'd flick myself in the cheek
every time I thought of you.

On the metro,
a commuter has your eyes.
-flick-

Grocery shopping;
maybe I'll make breakfast for dinner,
your favorite.
-flick.-

In bed,
cozied up in thigh socks and an old t-shirt.
Yours. Oops.
-flick, flick-

I flicked myself until my cheek was bruised
but still I thought of you.
I realized then
there wasn't much difference between
before you left
and now;

I'm hurting either way.

--Flick

Midnight
has never been for the content.

It is for lust and longing,
passion and anger,
salt and skin,
cold pillows wet with hot tears.

Why did we ever think
we could just be comfortable
at an hour made for witching?

--Midnight

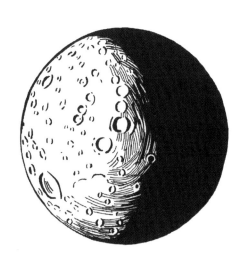

I spent so much time
wondering how I'd replace you
not realizing
you need not replace
a puddle of acid rain
when the whole ocean
is at your feet.

--Acid rain and oceans

You called me vanilla because I bored you, but have you ever smelled vanilla? Ever tasted it on the tip of your tongue, or smelled it on her collarbone as you kissed your way down to oblivion? Ever gotten it in ice cream for your sore throat because everything else made it scream? Have you ever swirled it into black coffee with milk and used it to cry away a hangover? So go ahead and call me vanilla. Maybe I'm boring, or maybe your palate is just a little unrefined.

--Vanilla

I shatter a lightbulb on the hardwood floor below the
picture window
and watch as the sunlight chooses a few shards at a time
to use as tiny prisms.

It reminds me of how
I seem to be able to love myself in pieces,
but never all at once.

--*Tiny prism*

Whoever said
an ugly truth
is better
than a beautiful lie
clearly never heard
-or felt-
your tongue form words.

--*Tongue*

1. Tell her how hard your life has been. How nobody in the world understood you until she came along. How she's *not like other girls.*
2. Tuck her into bed every night under blankets of sweet nothings and heart-eye emojis in her inbox. By the time she realizes the actions do not follow, she'll already think it's her fault.
3. Give her just enough attention to keep the thread intact. The thread is stretchy and thick; it can weather almost any wrongdoing.
4. Say you want to be with her forever, but don't make plans past next Saturday.
5. Tell her you love her over and over and over. Tell her *you are the only one who never gives up on me.*

--How women get stuck

Apologies fall from your mouth
like grease
staining your fingers
and everything you touch.

You disgust me.

--Three strikes, you're out

Kids are dying
and we're doing nothing.
We're bickering about right and left
and guns and mental health
and pointing fingers.

It's more than petty,
it's vile.

Vile because in a few months or weeks or days,
more innocents will die.
More future doctors and singers and humanitarians.

This wasn't what they meant by
Nothing gold can stay.

What they meant was
kids will have sex and try beer
and learn some mistakes cannot be undone.

Not *kids will die before they ever have a chance to live.*

--14 Feb 2018

You come and go as you please,
into my life and out.
A vagabond.

I tell you I can't do it anymore,
but we both know
I won't leave you in the cold
when half my bed
is empty.

--Vagabond

He said
I heard there was a sacred chord
and I stopped him right there
because I do not want
to be serenaded by a man
who cannot be bothered
to write his own song.

--Hallelujah

Every night
I stare out my window
hoping to see a smoke signal
rising up above the tree line,
but night after lonely night
the sky is as clear as you were
when you said
I'm not coming home.

--Smoke signals

One night I tripped on a rock
and fell the wrong way
up into the sky
with the clouds and the moon
and I saw you
missing me
the way I miss you.

- *The wrong way*

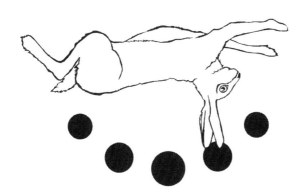

This year my hair grew longer and the space between us grew wider. A lover lost is a friend gained, but not for us. The tides came and went and came and went. Everything changed, except that which stayed the same. *Three, two, one!* The clock strikes midnight, and everyone cheers so I do too. Where are you? I cannot say. I only know that the fates are slowly untwining our lifelines and I can either miss you forever or learn to love myself.

I can learn to love myself.

I *will* learn to love myself.

--The New Year

Suck the venom out
and cauterize the wound.

Squeeze and burn
that man right out of you.

--When stitches just won't do

How many people
have begged the doctor
to save the gangrenous limb
hanging from their body;
the one slowly killing them?

You, my love,
are that gangrenous limb
and the time has come
to lop you off.

--Gangrene

I reached for you
like a baby
reaches for its mother
the very first time;

I'd never felt you,
but I knew I needed your love.

--*Instinct*

79

Finding you
was like searching the house
for my glasses, only to find they were on my head.

You were right there all along,
I only had to reach for you.

--Soulmate

He asked
if I wanted to play
Seven Minutes in Heaven
so I turned off all the lights,
put on the album version of
Champagne Supernova
and told him to hold me
like it was the end of the world.

--Champagne Supernova

PART 3

(Memories, like bullets)

nostalgia

nos-tal-jee-uh

--noun

1. A sentimental yearning for the happiness of a former time in one's life; for one's home or homeland; for one's family or old friends.
2. The songs that remind you of your high school friends. Remembering the rush of your first kiss. Old family pictures with all the cousins you never see anymore. The foods that taste like your favorite holiday. Gigapets. Pokemon. Smirnoff Ice and Zema in a sandpit. Watching *13 Going on 30* and realizing you now identify more with the thirty year olds than the teenagers. The smell of fall leaves that remind you of back-to-school. Freshly mowed grass. The little important things we took for granted that now mean everything because all we have left are the memories.

Origin: 1770 [New Latin, Greek] nost (a return home) + algia (suffering)

Remember when you were young?

When the world was flat
and your parents were still together
and the worst thing a person could do
was beat you to the last swing
on the playground?
When Pocahontas was a love story
not a kidnapping
and heartbreak was something
you'd only read about in books.
Before you knew growing up
is more than just staying up late
whenever you want;
that it is crying an awful lot
and never having enough money
to buy a couch
or brand-name peanut butter
or health insurance.
It's so easy to be naïve,
and oh,
how I miss those days.

--*When you were young*

85

Thank you for being there,
for not being one of the too-many
who are not.
Thank you for telling me
keep yourself special
but letting me figure out
what that meant.

--Dear Father

I can feel the universe
pulling at my insides,
stretching me like a fitted sheet
over the last mattress corner,
leading me this way
and that against my will.
I don't understand it
but then,
I don't get a say
in the affairs of
bedsheets and universes.

--Bedsheets and universes

My backbone
never worked very well.
I was trampled beneath
other people's feet
and made small
so I grew a second spine
which held my head higher
and could not be crushed so easily
by the words of men.

--Second spine

Oceans
and eyes
and indigo skies,
broken hearts
and blood without breath
and you ask
why my favorite color is blue.
My favorite color is blue
because blue is life
and the absence of it
and everything in between.

--Blue

Sometime last year
my womb woke up,
realized it was empty,
and started crying
the way the earth does
in the springtime
before the green comes.

--*Ticking clock*

I learned how to love
from two people
who knew how to love
and that has made
all the difference.

--Gratitude

It is so hard
to be decent sometimes.
To not hate his girlfriend,
for being so damn beautiful.
To not lay on the car horn
after that guy cut me off
just because it feels good.
And then there's the family
-yes family- that dig through the recycling
outside my complex every weekend.
Mom, dad, little kids.
I know they're going to come,
but I chuck my cans and bottles in with everything else
because it's easy.
But wouldn't it be just as easy
to leave them in a separate bag
with an anonymous note and a five-dollar bill
I'd probably spend on something I don't even need?

There is so much good
Within my reach
that I'm just not reaching for
and I don't know why.

--*I must try harder*

My father called me
tiger
instead of *princess*
so I grew up
with claws and teeth
and never believed I needed saving
from anyone but me.

--*Tiger*

My great fear
is that one day my children
will sit on my lap and say
read to me, mommy
one more book; please?
and we'll flip through dog-eared pictures
of blue whales and elephants and pangolins
the way I used to look at dinosaurs;

in wonder of great creatures that used to be.

--Extinct

95

When my toes are in the ocean
I cannot help but feel
my blood is more salt than iron
and my flesh is more water than skin.

--*Salt and iron*

He would get up early
to sprinkle foreign coins
on the beach
then wake us up
at sunrise.

Pirates,
he would say;
they came again.

And my sister and I
would run down the gravel path
barefoot
to pick up strange gold coins
believing in magic,
not knowing the magic
was him.

--Grandfather

I want my sons
to play with dolls.
I want them to use their
imaginations for empathy
so they never want
to use their hands for pain.

--Dolls

We talk about lost boys,
but where are all the lost girls?
All over the world,
they have been forced
to grow up at nine,
twelve.
fifteen.

You tell me;
where can they find
Neverland?

--Neverland

We're watching the evening news
in the living room.
World leaders with overactive ~~trigger~~ Twitter fingers
bickering about whose "button" is the biggest,
kids being shot every god-forsaken day
and everyone everywhere getting trophies
just for showing up and sort-of trying.

I wonder aloud how far we are from
ballerinas held down by blocks and blindfolds
and dog-whistles in our ears.
My husband
(who still reads the paper
because he's old fashioned like that)
just looks up at me,
sighs, and says

It's a doozy.

--Harrison Bergeron*

*A satirical short story written by Kurt Vonnegut in 1961.

Sometimes
listening
to the spaces between words
reveals more
than the words themselves.

--Mary

I dip my fingers into the tide pool,
feeling little shells
flee my wandering hands.
They slip right through
and burrow away
only to pop back up
as soon as I let go.

Will everything in life
remind me of the ones who left?

--Coquinas

102

I call him *little brother*
but he is bigger than I am
and probably smarter too.
I still remember holding him in the hospital,
bursting into tears because
ten-year-old me had never held anything so beautiful.
Seeing him all grown up aches a little;
nostalgia and pride all balled up in one.

I wonder why
there isn't a word
for a feeling like that.

--*Little brother*

Pain seems to stick in my gut and bleed out my fingers while I type, so here is a poem for all the good things I should write about more. The sunlight coming through my bedroom window on a weekend morning. The little dog who keeps me warm and licks my face when I cry. The monarch butterfly that reminds me of a friend I've never met. The drunken moments when I finally have the courage to tell the women in my life how beautiful they are. Kissing my best girlfriend on the lips just for the hell of it. The wedding built from love and sunshine and sacrifice. The days when the air doesn't feel so heavy (like right now). The ferocity of the winter and the green of every spring. The stillness of my heavy soul when I'm with him.

--The good things

You would hold out your arms
and say
do you know how much I love you?
And we would say
more than this
or as much as that,
but you were a goddess
and I think
no love was as great
as yours
for your creations.

--Mother

Let it be.
Let the waves crash
and the sun set
and the boy leave.
You cannot make
the Earth stop turning
when it wants to.

--Let it be

BELUGA

(A collection of short verse)

You are proof
that there is vulnerability
in even the brightest
of fires.

--Lindsay

You're a little sad
and that's okay.

You don't have to be
like the rest of them;
dark stars shine too

--Dark star

How do you know you're a goddess?

I cried oceans and did not drown.

Sometimes our captors live
in the places we call home.

Sometimes they live
in our hearts
and never set us free.

--Captors

Sometimes you have to burn bridges
just to keep yourself from going back
to where you started.

Sometimes controlled burns
are necessary for growth.

Just ask the trees.

Your sweat
tastes of the ocean;
come with me

to the sea.

--Innuendo

There is a difference
between speaking for someone
and helping someone be heard.

(Only one is about them)

--Ally

The tree swaying too far left
  is just as likely to snap
  as the tree swaying too far right.

  --Bipartisanship

Too many men are thieves;
borrowing time and never giving any back.

Broken
and broken in
are two completely different things
and you are neither.

You
are candy
when I know
I need fruit
but I am
an American girl
and I just can't resist
a little extra sugar.

--American girl

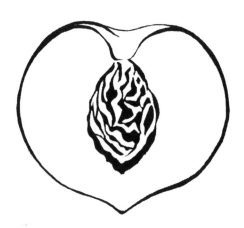

Achilles had a heel,

Paris had Helen,

Trojans had a horse

and I,

I have you.

--Tragic flaw

You are lucky if you have no idea who you are,
for you can still be anyone you want.

Would you still miss the sun if it burned out one day?
Or would you look for the same love in a different star.

Why does the moon make you cry?

Because she is everything that I will never be.

--Full

We wander,
we wonder,
we wait.

For what, we're never sure.

East to west,
between two oceans.

You'll find it,
even if it sometimes feels
like you won't.

--Sarah

You do not get to push me
out of the nest then take credit
for teaching me to fly.

--Little bird

His mouth is my favorite flavor;

I crave it all the time.

--Candy

It is not your job to determine
whether someone else is oppressed.

--Her hijab, her business

I trace constellations on his chest
like he is heaven
and I am a little girl
enamored by the night sky.

The bombs didn't kill us,
apathy did.

Love
is never feeling like you owe anything
but wanting to give everything
all the same.

This is a story of broken limbs and scratched up knees. Of first periods and first kisses and first mistakes. Of jumping naked into cold lakes with high school friends and talking about the future over campfires. Passing around clove cigarettes, tasting the smoke of freedom. This is the story of cheap wine and deep talks and long, wet kisses. Of growing up but feeling small, and realizing with freedom comes responsibility and college loans and no job that makes enough money to ever pay them off. The story of spending years with the wrong people, but years we'd never take back because they led us to the right ones. Of screaming at our brains and the air and life itself for weighing on us so heavily it's everything we can do to eat and sleep and make tears come when they're needed. Of living with our parents in our twenties, when we thought we'd be off on some great adventure.

But don't you see, this is the adventure. All of it; this story. And the most magnificent part?

This story is ours.

--For the Millennials, always

I am not brave,
but I very much try to be
and I think that is enough
for today.

--Affirmation

Thank you.

Also by Emily Byrnes:

A Strangely Wrapped Gift

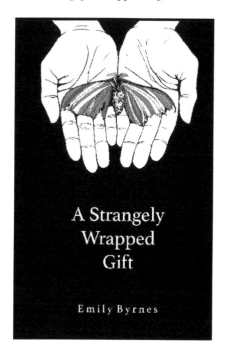

A debut poetry collection that follows a journey from mental illness and heartbreak to recovery, growth, and hope.. Available on Amazon.com and Barnes&Noble.com

Emily Byrnes can be found on Instagram and Facebook:
Facebook: @emilybyrnespoetry
Instagram: @emilybyrnes.poetry

Excerpts from *A Strangely Wrapped Gift:*

I am not the sunflower,
thrusting boldly toward the sky.

I am the seedling
pushing through the cracks
in the tennis court

and the wildflower
growing in the garden,
accidentally planted by the wind

and the water lily,
too short to break the surface
always fighting for the sun.

Growing is not easy for me;
I have never been a natural
but like nature,
I always find a way.

— — — — — — — — — — — — — — — —

It's okay
if sunlight strangles you,
if the air always feels too heavy,
and if walking out the front door
is scarier than a thousand hissing snakes.

137

Illustrator Lizzy Duga can be found on Instagram:
@pink_moon_illustrations

Made in the USA
Middletown, DE
24 March 2018